Somewhere,
a
Playground

Somewhere, a Playground

poems
by Rich Ferguson

MOON
TIDE PRESS

~ 2025 ~

Somewhere, a Playground

Editor-in-chief
Eric Morago

Operations Associate
Shelly Holder

Associate Editors
Mackensi E. Green
Ellen Webre
Alyssa Murray

Editor Emeritus
Michael Miller

Front cover art
Mark Wilkinson

Author photo
Mark Wilkinson

Book design
Michael Wada

Moon Tide logo design
Abraham Gomez

Somewhere, a Playground
is published by Moon Tide Press

Moon Tide Press
6709 Washington Ave. #9297
Whittier, CA 90608
www.moontidepress.com

FIRST EDITION

Printed in the United States of America

ISBN # 978-1-957799-33-9

I allow myself to dream of roses though I know the bloody war continues.

— Essex Hemphill

It's not until you sing in the key of tears
you realize all our bones have a story to tell, especially

                                        the broken ones.

They say wounds don't discriminate;
they're an equal opportunity

                                   destroyer.

Still, there's too much beauty and not enough bombs
for this movie of us to have an

                           apocalyptic ending.

If you ask me what the weather is like,
I'll say stormy with

                a chance of paradise.

Contents

Somewhere, a Grave

Somewhere, a Light

Somewhere, a Song

Somewhere, a Playground

Somewhere,
a
Ghost

Somewhere, a Playground

after Danez Smith

When bullets grew wings that day
and flew through school,
we thought it was the sound
of hammers falling.

Bad day to be a child,
printing upper and lowercase letters,
learning the cycles of the sun and moon,
and how to take turns.

Addition meant putting things together,
subtraction taking them away.

Bullet plus body equals blood.
Body minus blood equals gone.

But don't call us ghosts.
Don't think of our bodies in tiny caskets
with stuffed unicorns and plush puppies
forever unnamed.

Color us alive,
where bullets don't fly,
a playground filled
with monkey bar love,
children crisscross applesauce
beneath a tree,

breaking into pieces the words
of this big world,
sounding them out.

Bullet in a Bar

Somewhere there's a bullet in a bar wanting to tell you its backstory, how it was once a natural element, stable and copperkissed. Bullet wants to explain how human hands tore it from the earth, made blood become floor and the sky a whole big field of hurt. Bullet says it's fed up with being the steady beat of death's drum solo, tired of using hot tears to ink devil tattoos. Insomnia-ridden, ghost-haunted, its thoughts are a tangle of sirens and crime scene tape. Bullet says, make my next drink a double. Strike that. Make it a triple of lives returned from tombs. It would rather get lost in the bottle than crawl back into the barrel of a gun.

The Feels

That one call from jail will do little good when trouble is your only
next of kin. All your tongue wants to do is coat itself

in white-out and hide out: permanent hibernation in a white-noise
din. Bad juju in a pretty dress seems a far safer bet

than the horoscope you bought at the Dollar Tree and ended up
using as a brokeass drink coaster on the edge

of unmagical thinking. Should you say everything feels so heavy,
it's not hyperbole.

The clouds above look more like battlefields than a case of the
feels. As for the sky, blue is everywhere.

Blue like moods, like the edges of bruises. Blue like the truth that
goes blank when asked to state its name.

What St. Christopher Told Me
While Traveling Route 666

Utopia is going into foreclosure.

Utopia wears a Kevlar vest at all hours.

Utopia has a hair-trigger rage, shoots first and asks questions later.

Utopia is out of shape, can't touch its toes or do sit-ups.

Utopia has hidden agendas no TSA agent can detect.

Utopia got caught pouring battery acid into compassion's gas tank.

Utopia got caught transporting underaged idealism across state lines.

Utopia has transformed its zen garden into an Olive Garden.

When Utopia looks in the mirror, all it sees is dystopia.

Utopia refuses to offer room service in the heart's wounded hotel.

Utopia has a functional Ponzi scheme for every dysfunctional season.

Utopia has bones made of Muzak: it does the purgatory soft shoe.

Utopia has served jail time with all of Florida's banned books.

Utopia commits self-immolation believing it's the only way to
enlightenment.

Utopia hops the last train of thought out of town,
leaving the rest of us to pay all its bills and back taxes.

Utopia has forgotten how to cast the movie of a perfect life,
but is more than willing to cast the first stone.

Utopia writes its last will and testament in disappearing ink.

Utopia says there's something in the water, something in the air,
something in the way we're living that's making us lose our minds.

Utopia suffers from paranoia, despair, and disillusionment.

Utopia ain't what it used to be.

WildFire

WildFire is king on the killing floor. Mighty roar its mouth.
   All the ways it rages
             across the landscape.

Doesn't care about your skin color, religion, or what you do
   for a living.

         WildFire has an endless appetite.

      Can devour your possessions in just a few bites.

      Heathen and homewrecker.
        Malice in Assunderland.

Spark-footed erotica for arson escape artists.

        WildFire is a hunter. WildFire is a thief.

           WildFire is an addict.
           WildFire is grief.

WildFire says, "Touch me. Make it burn. Make it smoke. Make it ash.

Make it hurt."

Fire Head

When crouched down in the hills
surrounded by dried sagebrush
and golden wattle trees,
this is the story I imagine you tell yourself—

you were a colicky baby
breastfed on the babylonic.
Built by fist and broken home,
your mother was a junky,
your father, absent as the rent
that rarely got paid.

As a child,
you were a bedwetter,
a scrambled alphabet of loneliness,
your inner world a bone ghetto
surrounded by broken mirrors
and unmended fences.

As a teen,
whenever you stopped your lithium,
you were red-twitch
and phosphor-tongue,
smooth jazz
jammed into a light socket.

Then came that night
you ignited a downtown dumpster.
The contraction in your chest
when *I love you*
was spelled out in smoke.

From then on,
what held you together—

potassium chlorate oxidizer,
fuel like sulfur,
wooden splint cut from aspen,
a binder like glue
creating a head that ignited
when struck against a rough surface.

As for your head:

Fire head. Fire awarded. Fire cracked.

One way to open pleasure
to the light, with fire.
One way to lessen the pain,
burn everything around you.

Whenever that irresistible urge
tapped into your veins like fuel,
you were rocket-ready
to enact every dangerous desire.

Now,
crouched down in the hills,
surrounded by golden wattle trees
and dried sagebrush,
adrenaline drag races through your veins,
runs all stop signs.

Fever. Fervor.
Atlas of ignition.
Atman of ash.

You strike a match.
Your fingers like small rivers
bend around the flame,
cup it, keep it unmolested
by Santa Ana winds.

You pledge allegiance
to this flicker,
its yellow-mottled amber
seeping into your heart's
deepest blue.

You tell yourself
you are powerful, all-consuming,
that you can reduce
large areas of a lush and lavish city
to the dust
God chokes on.

What Good Conscience Says at the Dinner Table Between Mouthfuls of Light

Because the enemy sleeps with eyes open and heart closed.
Because our heads and hands don't always get along.

Because the belly of the beast sometimes resembles the interior of
our past apartments.

Because there's a memory tied around our finger that won't allow
us to forget
       the broken parts of our past.

Because it's hard for arms to embrace shadows,
because shadows sometimes wear our bodies
       better than we do.

Because wounds come in all shapes, sizes, and kisses. Because fire
is at the heart of our yeses, and yeses don't always survive the rain.

Because sometimes the only language we can skywrite in is
falling. Because falls don't always follow summers.

Because there aren't enough desert winds to eliminate sorrow's
footsteps,
       we continue to be that air
       in search of a clear blue sky.

Nights Whose Lips Taste Like Gasoline

Nights when the moon's got a kiss that tastes like it's been huffing gasoline. Nights when you can feel your heart stalled out at the

intersection of beloved and bedeviled. Shadowy hours when the clock's whiskey bottle offers another shot of been done wrong.

Murky moments when the call of pavlovian stars brings out the mongrel in us.

When the walls close in, when the walls close in—dear angels above, poke some holes in the sky

so we can breathe.

Somewhere,
a
Wound

The Sirens Have Been Screaming Lies About Us

The sirens have been
screaming lies about us;

those emergencies proclaiming
we're their bastard next of kin,
children of oblivion and broken glass;

worried wanderers
roaming pitiless cities
of demolished optimism;

our cold bones clattering
like a failed fortune teller's
shuffled deck of cards;

paralyzed predictions,
doom-age daydreams;

wounds unwound into paths
where we're crossed
and double-crossed
by black cats
engaged in hex trafficking.

The sirens
have been screaming lies about us;

claiming we've got bulletholes for eyes,
that our mind's white space
has been filled with suicide notes
scribbled in misery's ink;

that our every moment is spent
taping up the busted windows of shattered souls;

that our names
have adopted all the aliases of pain;

that we're as ravenous and raving
as terror's tied-off vein,
aching for a syringe of serenity
that'll never come.

Sirens wail a ballad shambles,
sirens make the word *flower*
sound like *murder,*
sirens unsheathe their knives,
slash the night with death cries.

The sirens
have been screaming lies about us;

that we're pimps and pariahs,
monotone messiahs
decked out in sallow-skinned promises
of raptureless tomorrows;

that our remaining graces
crossdress as annihilating angels;

that our scraps of good intentions
have been ravaged by mind traps,
kill cults, and outlaw death trips.

The sirens have been saying
we've got the keys
to the extinction machine;

that we're haters, hedonists,
heart arsonists
whose stuffed-down angers
are dry weeds in fire season,
begging for a match.

Sirens wail a ballad shambles,
sirens make the word *flower*
sound like *murder,*
sirens unsheathe their knives,
slash the night with death cries.

The sirens
have been screaming lies about us;

that deep within our chests
are burlap bags
packed with rabid dogs;

dogs howling, growling, foaming at the mouth,
dogs whose temperaments are built
from lost bets and the short end
of broken wishbones;

dogs craving the raw meat of gutterspeak
and bloodclot lullabies.

The sirens say
our inner weather
is thunderstorms
followed by swarms of torment;

that we're incurable cretins
tearing down Xanax edens,
that grief's got us on speed dial,
that our fantasies
got a date with the coroner on the street corner.

Sirens wail a ballad shambles,
sirens make the word *flower*
sound like *murder,*
sirens unsheathe their knives,
slash the night with death cries.

Some nights
those sirens are so loud
only tombstones
can sleep through it all.

A Gene for Tears

Even if you watch this country with the sound turned down,
all the venom and inequality still bruise through.

So many derangements arranged in strange and familiar ways.
Intoxicated logic. Unmended melodies with insufficient pills
or winning streaks to cross the finish line.

Even with the sound turned down,
you can still hear a cry take hold in the throat.

You understand how a battered soul knows its way around a
twelve-bar blues when jagged howls of fist verbs shatter the air.

Even with the sound down, a down sound, you can still hear how
some are beat so bad their spilled blood becomes jazz,

a music to hymn a broken body to heaven.

The Bullet Makes Its Case For Spirit Animal

I know what you think you want,
a creature with wings,
an eagle perhaps,
or a dove
that apologizes for the invention of war
whenever you bleed.

But I am what arrives
when everything else
lies perished, punished,
or is simply too slow.

Call me bullet—

the one fueled by
vengeance, velocity,
and a world
of reckless decisions.

I'm here to teach you
how to
move through life,
how to
derange and devour,
when you're starving
and broken.

I've witnessed the fall
of the Byzantine Empire,
armed the Ottomans,
reveled in the invention
of the slide-action and semiautomatic.
Bled my way through
two World Wars,
Korea and Vietnam.
Kent State and Columbine.
Port Arthur and Christchurch.

I've seared
through flesh and folklore,
shattered ribs and well-being.

I've filled mouths with regrets
whose taste
can never be spit away.

Call me bullet.

Allow me
to fill in the trenches
you've dug deep in your heart
to escape my name.

Allow me
to dance with your dread,
to propel your pulse
to 900 mph.

Why choose a spirit animal
who'll apologize
for their actions
or be weighed down
by guilt.

If you want to learn
how to hunger
without shame,
how to soar
towards what you want
without veering off course,

I'm your dreambreaker,
your ghostmaker.

If you survive me,
my memory will
still follow,
my teeth
clenched on nightmares
you're too traumatized to chew.

So embrace me,
place me on your tongue,
make me your brutal eucharist.

Know
that I understand
speed, intent,
the absolute physics of consequence.

I'll teach you
how to enter another
without asking permission;

how to
rupture, disengage,
how to live with decisions
you can never change.

And
on those nights you can't sleep,
when everything
smells like cordite and contempt,
when your brain is a trigger,
and your last breath
can't exit your body
fast enough,

I'll be right beside you,
whispering in your ear—

"aim true, or don't aim at all."

What the What

What confounds us.
What we know to the depths of our souls.
What makes the soles of our feet burn.
What our pain is, and what we do with it.
What we do for love.
What animals mate for life.
What weapons will look like in 100 years.
What our history of violence tells us.
What time whispers in our ear when another year slips by.

What slips between our fingers, between the cracks.
What cracks us up.
What gets us up out of bed every morning.
What we see when we look in the mirror.
What to do for a broken heart.
What to do if your what-if machine breaks.
What we can learn from our mistakes.
What we can learn from the color of a star.
What we wish for when we wish upon a star.

What truths are self-evident.
What our parents aren't telling us.
What our politicians aren't telling us.
What to do to cleanse your colon.
What to do to cleanse your soul.
What to take for a yeast infection, or erectile dysfunction.
What a dangling or misplaced modifier looks like in a sentence.
What a prison inmate's life sentence costs the average taxpayer.

What it costs to build a house.
What it costs to buy a house.
What Lincoln said about a house divided.
What Shakespeare said about destiny and the stars.
What scars we wear proudly.
What wounds we keep hidden deep.
What we've lied about, rioted about.
What we've remained absolutely quiet about.
What the coroner's report will say about us when we're gone.
What our families, friends, and coworkers will say about us when
we're gone.

What to do to get turned on.
What to do when you're turned off.
What made Van Gogh cut off his ear.
What paint colors go together or make people look more beautiful.
What it really means when people say beauty is in the eye of the
beholder.

What eye color is most sensitive to light.
What it takes to power Times Square.
What 9/11 looked like from outer space.
What you can and can't take on airplanes.
What you can and can't buy with food stamps, or eat while pregnant.

What role folic acid plays in pregnancy.
What acid taught Timothy Leary.
What we should and shouldn't be leery of.
What agitates us, brings us peace.
What meditation does to the brain.
What cancer does to the brain.
What we know about wisdom vs. intelligence.
What we know about ignorance vs. stupidity.
What stupid things people do with their smartphones.

What women do that drive guys crazy.
What guys do that drive women crazy.
What it really means when a guy says he's scared.
What it really means when a woman says, *"Fine."*
What degree of separation you are from Tom Waits vs. Tom Cruise.
What your musical taste or taste in movies says about you.
What the chicken says when crossing the road.
What we've done for kicks on Route 66.
What 666 means to a mathematician vs. a devil worshiper or biblical scholar.

What prayers to say for abundance, what prayers to say for healing.
What we've held in our hands.
What we'll be handing over to the next generation.
What we've handed over as a bribe, peace offering, or evidence.

What the witness saw.
What the victim saw.
What the shooter saw when staring down the barrel of his rifle.
What we see when looking up at the clouds.

What we see when looking down deep into ourselves.

Garden of Eden Now Bleedin'

Remember when we shared
the same breath and were one?

When we shared a language
that defied hungry ghosts,
or when we swam together
in wild waters that could not drown us?

Since our fall from grace,
we have lost kinship with innocence.
We have experienced so many variations
of original sin
that its taste has become far from original.

These paradises
we have burned and abandoned
have collapsed into a Garden of Eden now bleedin'.
A complex geometry
where parallel lines
of love and consideration
contend with irrational proportions
of emotional, physical neglect and constriction.

Non-complementary angles
of sexism versus fairness.
Those seeking domination battle it out
with those seeking collaboration
in the multi-dimensional arena
of our human condition.

When seeking union between the sexes,
one must learn to transform
opposition into empowerment,
cruelty into congruency.

Create ratios of respect.
Equilateral equality.
A perfect circle,
one that unifies,
strives to heal this wound of being human,
for we are quick to anger, slow to heal.

Dragging our inner rivers for the body of evidence
to free us
from the gridlocked and mindlocked madness
of our Garden of Eden now bleedin'.

The place where one confuses
the highly personal with the universal,
retunes enlightenment to a TV reality
where we can't stop looking at our phones,
even when in the presence of redemption.

In our Garden of Eden now bleedin',
hear the gunfire and continual cry of sirens.
Witness our struggles
to grow beyond our insanities and instabilities—

new bones sprouting from old burdens.
Psyches surviving alley fights
with a world gone rogue.

Carving intellects sharp enough and weapon enough
to save ourselves from the dangerous primal instincts
breeding in our Garden of Eden now bleedin'.

That we may one day untether ourselves
from this mothership of mayhem.
Float off into harmonic stardust,
witness ourselves in the cracked-mirror moon;
realizing that, despite it all,
we have the potential
to become beautiful and unbroken.

That beyond our Garden of Eden now bleedin'
our flowers of good fortune can flourish
even as our world devolves into deserts of destruction.

That we can sleep with fire
and wake up the right kind of bright.

That we can return to innocence and from innocence to shadow.
That we can return to shadow and from shadow to river.
That we can return to the river and from the river to the crossroads.
From the crossroads to song, from song to heart.
From heart to a home
where a new union between man and man,
woman and woman,
man and woman blossoms.

Souls guided by plant instinct,
tenacious in the desire to rise.
Root voice, a journey from oblivion into brilliance.
Our seed smiles, a multiplying joy.

In our new Garden of Eden no longer bleedin'
remember to let the roses grow,
but pull away the weeds
before they tower over us
on this spinning ball of eroding and beautiful blue.

Somewhere,
a
War

13 Ways of Looking at They

I
Upon waking, they don their masks of hate.

II
They squeeze off endless rounds
from their .357 Magnum Opus of Obliteration.

III
For breakfast, they eat serial killers.

IV
For lunch, they eat the hearts of the good-intentioned.

V
Firebombing churches is their one true religion.

VI
They roll around in shit and mud,
then claim they're cleaner
than everyone unlike them.

VII
They're not your friend
until you're dead,
and even then, their allegiance is only temporary.

VIII
They breathe, sleep, and eat guns.
They fuck guns. They have gun babies,
then send them out into the world
to seriously fuck with you.

IX
The only thought on their minds:
how to add a 666th Amendment to the Constitution.

X
Fascism is their only form of humanism.

XI
They unimagine the sun,
feed lilies handfuls of sleeping pills.

XII
Poison is their prayer,
the snapping of your neck, hymn.

XIII
Nihilism is the highway they drive
to get from one moment to the next.

Dear America,

Where are your papers to show your citizenship?
What are your thoughts on democracy?

America, your erogenous zones have become hot-button issues.
Your blood is poisoned with racism, radicalism, misinformation,
and political polarization.

America, stop melting down rounds to make crowns for your molars.
Stop building playgrounds for new Hitler youth.

And what about your thoughts on education? Can you read my
letters
or calculate the difference between your richest and poorest citizens?

Dear America, is that a knife in your back? A ticking bomb
beneath your powdered wig? Your pork-barrel politics are stuffed
with trichinosis. Your eyes have gone freedom blind.

Dear America, why haven't I heard back from you? Are you in
prison?
If so, I'll send you a cake with a pen inside
         so you can write back.

Open Letter to Human Existence

To the bloated bureaucrats and plutocratic cut-throats.
To the wannabe dictators and coronated kings of fist parades.

To the fear mongers and panic peddlers, the book burners and
history unlearners. To the jackboot tramplers of zen gardens.

To the composers of nail-in-the-soul melodies, and
to those who seek financial gain from our tragic pain.

To the death squads and dream poachers, slave traders
and day traders of hate.

To all of you, I say—

no man is truly our master
when there are wild and singing wolves in our hearts.

Random Text Message Threads Where the Devil Tried to Lure Me to Hell

Hey Rich, we've restocked our shelves with your favorite Robert Johnson records! This is only for a limited time. We look forward to seeing you soon! – D.

Hi Rich, we regret to inform you that today's session with your therapist has been canceled due to an emergency. Not to fret! One of our trained psychopaths can see you at any time. We look forward to hearing from you soon – D.

Dear Rich, this is a payment reminder for your credit card ending with XXX2168. Pls. follow the link to obtain directions to our facility so you can pay in person – D.

Rich, you have an appointment with Dr. Dante today at 3 PM. Please arrive at 18 Lake Cocytus Ave., Mt. Purgatory Hospital. 10 mins. prior – D.

Hi Rich, don't forget your massage is today at Sheol Salon. Please arrive with your flame-retardant suit – D.

One War

bleeds into another war where everyone bleeds
a little more than the war before.

What happens to a war deferred?
Does it sugar sweet or heavy love then run?

Maybe it just dreams like sun.

A Confection of Chaos and Glory

Life teeters on a fulcrum
between melody and madness.

A confection of chaos and glory
stuck between the teeth.

Some salvage old kisses from love's cemetery
and polish them anew,

while others rub malice and menace into wounds
and call it medicine.

Walking the world's streets,
you can feel the mixed-message braille

of broken glass
and heads-up pennies beneath your feet.

The chalk outline of a body here, a bouquet of laughter there—
a teetering between melody and madness.

You can feel it in each new earthquake and bomb blast.
Yet even in the most violent moments, when grace dies,

its hair refuses to stop growing.

Somewhere,
a
Grave

When That Knocking at the Door Sounds
a Lot Like Death

I wonder if we ever become allergic to ghosts or just the dirt
from their graves.

When death arrives at my door, I don't imagine it bearing a
bountiful bouquet

as the living are generally the ones who lay fresh blossoms
upon burial mounds. The number of those who've passed away

must surely outnumber my remaining brain cells. Eventually,
those, too, will become dirt and dust.

But not before I remember those who've left us. Sometimes
this world can break my heart.

Other times, love is enough to remind all ghosts
they need not be allergic to us.

The Superstitious Cemetery

There's a superstitious cemetery filled with four-leaf clovers and lucky pennies. It forbids yellow flowers, as they're calling cards for infidelity and separation. Believes people should hide their thumbs when passing to protect their parents from death. Doesn't allow its occupants to sleep with their heads to the west. Refuses to walk under ladders or toast with water, even if it's holy. Steers clear of chain letters and chewing gum at night. Carries a rabbit's foot in its pocket and crosses its fingers when wishing the dead a peaceful rest. Once the superstitious cemetery asked if it could be the narrator of my life story. I didn't know how to respond.

Awkward silences mean an angel is passing by.

When the Truth Serum Hadn't Completely Kicked In

When I say it's a sunny day, what I mean is, it's raining frogs.

When I say it's quiet outside, what I mean is, isn't that the sound
of Nero's fiddle?

When I say everything will be OK, what I mean is, it looks like
history
is practicing its blindfolded knife-throwing trick again.

When I say listen to the world sing in the key of life, what I mean is,
our earth is moaning a vertigo boogie
          that sends our souls reeling.

When I say I do my best to look on the bright side of life, what I
mean to say is,
there are days when my inner child should be
          named Tolstoy.

Why I Hate the DMV

It's not the tepid bathwater disposition
of the DMV worker as they tell you
to take a number, then be seated;

It's not that there are only two employees
to assist the twenty-five people in front of you;

It's not the basement of hopelessness
you feel trapped within,
along with all the other people
trying to renew their license,
obtain a registration, perform a notice of transfer
and release of liability.

The worst thing about the DMV is having your picture taken.

Every year
you look more and more like your father.
The tired eyes, the additional lines
around your nose and mouth,
the hairline retreating
into a deeper widow's peak.

Each new license photo
is a wanted poster for your DNA,
the deep-down villain,
killer of contentment,
the vicious salt scrubbed into the sinful wounds
of the father and son.

The genetics of abuse
passed down through belt beatings and beratings.
Your father's words,
the inverse of bells,
insisting you get your head out of the clouds,
how dreaming will never put food on the table.

As a child, you swallowed it all
like burnt TV dinners,
believing it was the only meal
you deserved.
But once your teenage years
served up a taste of rebellion,
you spit the pain back in your father's face
with a firm *Fuck You.*

But now you're older.
You see it in the photo,
how you've become a citizen
of your father's hurts and anger.
The shared breakdowns—

lost jobs, lost friends, a broken marriage.
How each new failure has brought you closer,
your lives a buddy road trip running on four flat tires.

When your number is called,
you hope your next license photo
will look more like your better self
or at least a little less
like the defeated version of your father.

As you stand before the camera,
you try to cut him some slack,
try to cut yourself some slack.

What the Child Witnessed in the Cinema of His Mother's Eyes

the movie of a breakdown
spun in reverse
ashes gathering
forming a crumpled body,
body rising healthy and shining
walking backwards into
a new tomorrow moving forwards

In the All-Night Bar of Insomnia

moonlight moonlights as a lounge singer.

Wolves are the bouncers, their howls packing more punch than
Socrates hemlock.

On the dance floor, wide-awake nightmares bully and brawl
to the sounds of cacophony's jukebox.

Grief's tears wipe ashtrays clean.

Regrets trade war stories in a corner booth.

In insomnia's all-night bar, delayed reflexes and mood disorders are
regular customers.

The hours tick by dizzily as if time has huffed the stalled clock's
gasoline fumes.

You can tip moonlight as it croons another sad tune, but that won't
get you closer to sleep.

Suspended in this Eden of inverse mercy, it's best not to suck up to
the bartender.

He's got a special drink tasting of gravity and the grave.

once again, i find myself wide awake in this bed—

this temple of turmoil, monastery of misery, memory foam
conjurer of unwanted memories; this off-switch to sleep onset,
rotted mausoleum of one-night stands minus a thousand; this zoo
of doom, crusher of circadian rhythms, hypnotizer of sleep-wake
cycles, cult of cranium derangements, dreamless spank machine,
peddler of sleep placebos, pimp of dirty needle parades; this
sophocles wash cycle, pallet of greek tragedy, dante's inferno with
a pillowtop, rimbaud's drunken boat without any oars to escape
snarling behemoths and blue immobilities; this sandman massacre
scene, bloated corpse of corporeal punishment, diddler of forty
winks, snotwad of snoozelessness, scheme of rusted innersprings;
this pale corral of hyperarousal, jittery flotation device on seas of
disorientation, tragic magic carpet traveling across multiple time
zones of alone; this tightly wound jack-in-the-box of sleep apnea,
frozen outpost of fight or flight, epicenter of algorithms of anxiety;
these 20,000 griefs under the sea armed with a string of weaponized
zzzzzz's; this hyperheaven of rapid breathing, massage parlor of
mixed affective states, negator of relaxation; this cage of rage,
googler of blues, grotto of no, std of unease, rv of ptsd; this
locomotive of instability, batmobile of imbalance, tram ride to
slamtime, 911-crankcalling calm breath robber counterfeiting
conundrum after conundrum wrapped inside still another
conundrum stuffed with lootbags of car alarms; this cinema of
backaches, enigma of pin cushions, second skin of jitters, cursive
writing master of sleepless ink; continual sink drip in hell's
kitchen; this ambien labyrinth 3:13 a.m. bus ride to nowhere;
insomnia bombgarden with a god complex; womb of tombdom,
anthem of brambles, dive bar for piranhas, open mic for maniac
jackhammers—

this bed, this bed, this head, this dread, this way station
between sun and moon that won't let me sleep.

Interview With the Blues

Should you ever
go on a job interview for the blues
and it asks you to describe yourself,
let it know your informal attire
means you're formally tired

of feeling on the skids with misery.

That your real job
is to remain aligned and upright,
outta sight of anything doing with

the short end of the winning stick.

When the blues asks
how you learned about the position,
say you heard it from
the jackbooted foot of woe,
its leather tongue flapping
a hymn of hurt

as it kicked you to the curb.

When the blues asks
about aspirations, tell it
you don't plan on forever
being the centerpiece of misery,
won't tango with a stranglehold.

When the blues asks
when you can start,
tell it you were actually

waiting for it to end.

Somewhere,
a
Light

3 a.m. Waffle House Waitresses

On nonstop solo cross-country drives, as one lonely day bleeds
into the next,

one encounters the 3 a.m. Waffle House waitresses.

Some sport a ring on their marriage finger; others have rough, bare
hands
worn from carrying full trays or doing dishes

when the washer calls in sick.

Some are tank-tough, old-school cool. Others have Moon Pie eyes
and sticky-sweet lips like candy wrappers.

Their apron pockets: stuffed with insufficient tips

and too much shit talk and gossip from drunks and locals. They'll
go home with the smell of kitchen grease and grits all over them.

Blessed Light For the Dying

To bud, to bloom, to dismantle miseries into melodies. To change murder to myrrh. To touch the void, leave our fingerprints upon stars.

To sing, to seek, to rosary old stones. To regale and re-gild tired sunrises.

To scatter worries for the birds feasting on hard times. For the ones flying south in winter, scatter hopes so joys may expand.

Cloud Flower

Look above. Lend the sky your ears.
Airy clouds burst into aria.

They form a cotton candy chorus line,
cavort across a vast blue stage.

The radio says a storm is coming our way.

The radio says that between us, there isn't
enough light in our pockets to ward off night.

Look above. The clouds can be anything we dream—
crow, castle, daisy.

Daisy.

Even Frankenstein was fascinated by flowers.

Born From a Womb of Fugitive Ghosts

The night our dreams crossed paths in our sleep, I played the water
guitar, and you washed old rainbows from your clothes.

You put an ear to the train tracks and told me the sunrise express
would soon arrive.

I mentioned how I'd been born from a womb of fugitive ghosts
but was attending night school to earn a degree in being more
comfortable in my skin.

You collected crow wings, sewed them to our old wounds
so they could leave us be.

I asked what it felt like to step into the shadow of our higher
selves. You said, here, let me show you.

Then you cut down all the trees in the forest of darkness
so we could better see the blossoms of gathering bright.

Paint It Black

There's a crow in my soul that's instinct-keen and mystic-winged. When I'm lonely, it joins me at karaoke bars singing, "Paint It Black."

It redesigns my soft insides into deserts, seacoasts, tundras, and rocky cliffs. Whenever I encounter a cruel individual, my crow teaches me never to forget that face.

When I say there is murder in my soul, I'm only referring to those times when my crow invites its kin over to party. Some evenings when I'm low, my soul crow tells me,

"Imagine moonlight falling like liquid diamonds at your feet. Imagine two floors down from your lips, there's someone yearning to kiss you."

Ways to Write a Poem

Listen with your eyes wide open.
Be votive candle, cloud diary,
an offering for heart and sky.
Should the pills you've consumed
hum your blood blind,
feel your way
to the metaphor dance floor.
At any moment,
should Lucifer's guitar feedback,
go higher in your reverb mind,
echo the words
'til the planet's poles reverse
and your inner walls melt away.
If the text weeps,
it's only your wounds
you have yet to heal.
Stay present within the orbit
of ink-smudged satellites.
The words you adore,
make them strange.
Odd words, love them up.
Sweat it out. Dream it out.
Sacrifice the images
that don't adorn
your higher angels
with vestiges of light.
They are beasting bones
to burn on cold nights.

What If?

What if coyotes conducted philharmonic orchestras?

What if birds knew us by name, and we knew them by their most cherished refrain?

What if honeysuckles were an unending mantra for our nostrils?

What if Starbucks changed its name to Influx and only served poetry flows?

What if cancer headed out to pasture?

What if dementia receded into a memory of itself?

What if the wolves outside our door went on a hunger strike?

What if, in the court of life, we could achieve great things even before a jury of our fears?

What if lightning storms were the sky's way of saying bright ideas are still possible, even in the darkest moments?

After Our Collective Heart Became a House Fire

After being caught between
        knuckle and nuance,
spitting out bloodied teeth
        and shreds of sensibility.

After we've whispered
        the name of our country
like curse and cure.
        After mistaking rupture

for rapture and exit for exist.
        After we've stuffed all our love
and differences into a time capsule,
        telling ourselves we'll revisit them

on our deathbed—after and before
        all this, there was a battle
so brittle it broke down
        to peace.

Fugitive Music

Sometimes I'm kept up late at night by love and death playing
double or nothing beneath my bedroom window.

Sometimes I sneak into cemeteries at night and sleep spooning
a tombstone so I'll know the feel of death when it comes.

If you ask me to tell you a story, I may start by saying, *once upon
a breathing river*, because sooner or later good fortune flows our way.

I was once a fugitive from a piano chain gang. You shoulda heard
the song I played that night of my great escape.

Somewhere,
a
Song

The Wounded Piano

Where the freeway crowds against a sidestreet, which trades dirty secrets with an alleyway, you'll find a wounded piano. It sings of what is gone and what remains. Old currency is stitched into its wayward notes. Meaningless to some, its tone is priceless. The music: ragtorn and rare, a glissando of heartbreak and radiance. Its melodies sparkle in the sunset hour. You can hear them over the highway's rush-hour sigh: cycles of static, cycles of singing.

All Music Is Related to Other Music

Brit punk moshes with honky-tonk.
Louisiana blues trade pains with opera.

Rockabilly shares fashion tips with grunge. Cybermetal sweats and
swears alongside psychedelic
in a crowded club
        while barbershop zones out on acid trance.

All music is related to other music.

Latin house flows into downtempo. Drum and bass hardstep
darksteps, sweat out chillwave
glitch. Glitch goes electropop,   blasts off into space rock.

Space rock floats back down to earth just in time to catch
freak folk trying out a freestyle rap in the dirty South.

All music is related to other music.

Agrotech laughs at all of cool jazz's jokes.
Samba invites doom metal over for Sunday dinner.

New age flirts with symphonic. Symphonic likes to crossdress
as reggaeton while trip-hopping
        through neo-soul.

No music is ever silent unto itself.

At the Karaoke Bar of Can't We All Just Get Along

At the karaoke bar of Can't We All Just Get Along, you won't find chair-hurling neo nazis or apish clans of police officers brawling to beat the last good chorus from your breath. What you will witness is a white suburban accountant with a receding hairline and dad belly performing Afroman's "Crazy Rap" to exorcise his implicit and explicit racial intolerance and lack of understanding for those walking on the wild side. You'll hear a fifteen-year-old buzz-cut lesbian sing Sinatra's "The Way You Look Tonight" in a radical act of self-love and acceptance. A former beauty queen performs a duet with a disabled Vietnam vet to confront her issues of beauty bias. A 12-year-old African-American girl will absolutely slay Dax's "Black Lives Matter" to cope with the trauma of her father being gunned down by a Ryan Palmeter wannabe. At the karaoke bar of Can't We All Just Get Along, all voices are accepted.

Even in their lowest and most ragged tones, there's pure gold.

What Is the Counterpoint to Sorrow-Torn Tears?

A radio tune in the key of uplift is a good place to start.

Or a flash mob of fireflies on a summer night.

A reveille of reverie ain't bad.

Even better, let's have better homes and gardens of happy hormones.

Gimme-gimmes of sweet-love shimmy.

A Monday hello in its Sunday best.

A long-tressed sky with rainbow highlights.

When balled fists fire off right-ons instead of fights.

When the pursuit of happiness flips the script and runs after you.

When lush new romantics offer good riddance to old heartbreaks
shaken, stirred, and poured over a future of optimistic ice.

At 7th & Esperanza

A man lives in a cathedral of begonias. On the piano, he plays
a telegram to a long-gone ineffable emotion.

The man has a daughter.

The young girl has new wings fastened to her shoulders with
ribbons and wishes. She dances as her father plays piano.

On the street, rain doubles
as holy water when the city's lucky number comes calling.

A drenched woman walks by. Her eyes have gotten into a bar fight
where both sides lost.

She hears the piano music and pauses. It's the sweetest sound she's
ever heard—starlings and sunshine, pearls and paper tulips.

She closes her eyes. As she does so, she notices something she's
never seen before: the instructions on how to survive
a crash-landing written on the inside of her eyelids.

Now, she can read them in the dark.

Everywhere I'm Not

When you were nouveau in New York, I was way too far west of cool.

When I was stoned and stumbling stupid along Amsterdam canals,
you were back across the Atlantic raging immaculate in a rock band.

When you were in the Orient, I was disoriented by L.A.'s rush
hour traffic.

When I was out on a limb, wailing "The Boys are Back In Town,"
you were "Closer to Fine" with the Indigo Girls.

When you were visiting infinite bliss, I was on a slow trolley to
melancholy.

When the moon was my last coin to pay my way through the night,
you had the morning sun for a third eye.

When you were everywhere at once,
I was just getting to know myself right where I stood.

What I Confessed to Ophelia
on Our First and Only Date

My heart is a lava lamp.

My heart is an electric chair.

My heart has hidden agendas that even I can't decipher.

My heart is seventh heaven.

My heart refuses to dine on canned laughter.

My heart carves itself into a pill then consumes itself.

My heart has bruised knees from continually genuflecting in the
chapel of longed-for happily ever afters.

My heart drunk dials the moon when I'm sleeping.

My heart has been mistaken for a crystal ball. It has been mistaken
for a grenade.

My heart is a horizon of bright hellos. My heart turns shadow
whenever it has to say goodbye.

My heart is a muscle that's way too insecure to pump iron at
Venice Beach.

It loves to beat, beat, beat. It loves to get down.

My heart has this thing about playing air drums to James Brown.

A Rock of Ages

In celebration of the documentary "Rock & Roll Made in Mexico"

In the beginning—

cosmic vibrations;
atoms joining atoms,
creating stars, universes,
acoustic waves of planets spinning,
galaxies coalescing, crashing,
ultrasounds and infrasounds
of the Big Bang
resounding across time and space.

Blank pages of age-old silences
rewritten by Earth's new formation

river movements
forming flowing meditations

dinosaur roar,
trees' green laugh,
first human hands
striking stone against stone,
sparking fire, fury, war cry.

Prehistoric music, Native American
and Aboriginal music
reverberating through the ages,
shamanic sounds
oscillating with onomatopoeia—

buzz, boom, growl

Ancient tones
scribed into song,
cuneiforms composed in harmonies of thirds:
three bones in the human ear,
three stars in Orion's belt,

of the people, by the people, for the people.

Folk music, Greek music, Muslim music,
songs of deliverance,
songs of heritage and remembrance,
intonations training prophets
and everyday people
to vocalize mosaics of chorus and cadence,
aural artworks painted on air.

Enduring compositions
outlasting
the fall of the Roman Empire,
the Medieval and Middle Ages,

imprisonment transformed into enlightenment,
a renaissance of polyphony and euphony,
tongues constructing templed time signatures
reviled and revered
through
Baroque, Classical,
and Romantic periods,

right into
a 20th-century revolution
where new technologies
captured and enraptured new freedoms
and experimentations
in musical styles and mediums.

Whole notes, half notes,
eighth and sixteenth notes,

all musical notes
leaning into one another
creating songs written and rewritten
with diverse lyrics and beats
yet still sharing the same electricity
beneath the skin.

The place where
rupture becomes rapture
and muscle memory
mimics memorable melodies
in a sweet choral repetition,
a listening deep within the body,
into the soul of rock and roll—

buzz, boom, growl

1950s American movies
bringing soundtracks
south of the border,
raucous reverberations
of Bill Haley and Elvis Presley
celebrated over Mexican radio.

Those sonic vibrations
transformed into rarified
and reinvigorated transmissions:

Cesar Costa
singing Spanish versions
of American hits,
Gloria Rios
dancing boogie steps
with rock beats.

In
café cantantes
and tardéadas,

Los Hooligans
Los Sparks
Los Locos del Ritmo

Lalo Toral
Johnny Ortega
Irma Estrada

El Pistón
cracking open
the canned heat,
El Brujo
flashing technicolor ambiance
of rhythm and blues.

These were not rebels
without a cause,
when their greater cause
was to rock and roll—

buzz, boom, growl

Loudspeaker prophets
and reverb's proverbs
wailing social and political messages
heard by '60s youth
in funky holes,
abandoned cinemas and parking lots
outside city limits.

Street demonstrations
railing against oppression,

songs of protest,
songs of healing breath,
man and woman-made melodies,
a Morse code of hope and howl
pulsing on air.

Harmonic crescendos
building bridges over
oblivion's bottomless pit;

shackles becoming the crackle
of riot's guitar amp
cranked well beyond ten—

buzz, boom, growl

Mexican rock
growing out its
government-cut hair,
former revolutions offering new revelations,
breaking free from the underground:

Caifanes
La Castañeda
Fobia
Café Tacuba

Songs singing seasons of new invention—
a weather as varied from good day sunshine
to heavy metal thunder.

Bombs and brutality
can't beat down this beat
for too long
because rock
is always gonna do
what it does best,

rise, baby, rise

Electrified or unplugged,
rock transforms
the I into We,
solitude into multitudes.

Our ears cleansed
with soundwaves
of holy-water wattage
rolling through the ages;

a rock of ages,
a rock of solid rock and roll.

Breath Is Music

Human steps are music. Choruses sewn from every thread of existence.

DNA blows blissful sax riffs. Eardrums hum, hearts lay down steady beats.

Lips bebop, feet hip-hop.

Human touch plays double-dutch with hanging ropes, twists them into love knots of well-tuned hopes.

Breath is music. Human steps are music. Hollers of tolerance break down horror-hewn walls.

B-natural beauty chimes timeless melodies.

The nectar drawn from human pain creates enduring voices sweet as rain.

Breath is music. Human steps are music. Choruses sewn from every thread of existence.

Live and Die in L.A.

I'm built from Tongva plant medicine and psilocybin-powered sound bath ceremonies. The amped-up grit and glitz of the Sunset Strip: from the living electricity of Jim Morrison at the Whisky à Go Go to River Phoenix's deep dive into overdose at the Viper Room.

My bones have been broken by car crashes, Starwood punk-rock mosh pits, and the 1943 Zoot Suit Riots. My skin has been fleshed by bits of shells, tiles, soda bottles, mirrors, and shards of pottery embedded in the Watts Tower spires.

I'm earthquake and handshake. Heartbreak and that big break. My veins move through me like Laurel Canyon's paisley-bricked and bougainvillea-lined road running from Sunset to the Valley, reverberating song cycles of Neil Young and Joni Mitchell.

Built by this city / blood and breath of the city / live and die in L.A.

My DNA luxuriates in cryofacial thermal shock float tank bliss imprinted with Moon Juice Super You. The tragedy and tears of the Cecil Hotel, the bebop rapture of Louis Armstrong at the Cotton Club, and the moment of genius when Mingus decided to drop the cello and take up the bass.

I'm wildfires and Richard Pryor freebasing. Ketamine therapy and colorful sneakers. Malibu beaches and Melrose boutiques. Retro glamour meets modern edge. Fusion cuisine and Lincoln Heights Latino history.

I'm the Runyon Buddha, Angels Flight, and Biddy Mason's free papers. Little Persia to Panorama City, Baldwin Hills to Boyle Heights. At Florence and Normandie, I gather bruises, cinderblocks, and beer bottles, transform them into sustainable jewelry of healing gestures.

Built by this city / blood and breath of the city / live and die in L.A.

I'm DTLA young monied hipsters and the aging homeless. Wild gardening and anti-depressant interior decorating. Radiohead supersonic soaring the Bowl. Miles Davis grounded at LAX for possession.

I'm 27th Street Bakery sweet potato pie. Sweat and panic in angular sunglasses trying to look more movie star than maniac. A down-and-out angel released from Men's Central Jail, now doing double shifts at the feather factory to earn new wings.

I'm street gangs and street racing. The romp and stomp of the Silverlake dog park. My heart is always open like Canter's Deli. I've been healed by Phil Spector's wall of sound and broken by his wall of guns.

Built by this city / blood and breath of the city / live and die in L.A.

I cruise the airwaves like Rodney on the ROQ. Old-school cool like the Rat Pack and Musso and Franks. I'm Beyoncé dining at Stella. Zoë Kravitz drinking at Delilah. Ice baths and espresso, Bodhi Trees and power yoga.

I'm rising rents and unaffordable housing. Striking actors, writers, and teachers. Dodger southpaw Clayton Kershaw striking out batters. Panting pit bulls and police reports. Archived deep cuts, knife cuts, and all kinds of cults.

I'm as promising as an Echo Park Lake sunrise. Durable as Buster Keaton's star on the boulevard. As lasting as psychic wounds reverberating from Japanese internment camps. I'm the road leading from the Hollywood Forever Cemetery and its celebrated dead, whose ghostly inflections are used as otherworldly driving directions.

Built by this city / blood and breath of the city / live and die in L.A

Somewhere,
a
Playground

Cinderella of the Audio Ball

While walking my students to recess, I notice one of my fifth-grade girls wearing a Nirvana T-shirt. I ask if she's ever heard of the band. She shakes her head no. I grab my phone, pull up YouTube. "This is one of their most famous," I say. "'Smells Like Teen Spirit.'" This makes my student giggle. She's transfixed by how the song's chunka-chunka guitar and thunderous drum intro bottoms out to a whisper during the verse. As Kurt Cobain sings, I tell my student, "He was a great songwriter. A great singer." My student notices my use of the verb *was* and offers a curious look. "He's no longer with us," I say. "He took his own life." "That's sad," my student says. I agree. "I wish he were still with us," I say. "He would've written so many more great songs. He would've had so many more great things to say." We continue watching the video, mesmerized as Cobain intones, "Hello, hello, hello, how low." During this quiet part, I tell my student, "Wait for it. Pretty soon things are gonna get loud." My student's eyes widen. The song's tension continues building. "Hello, hello, hello, how low…" Again, I tell my student, "Wait for it…" When the raucous chorus finally avalanches us, my student and I are beaming like we've got bells in our blood. "So, yeah," I say, pointing at her Nirvana tee. "That's a great shirt." My student glances down at the band logo, smiling like she's the newly crowned Cinderella of the audio ball. "Thanks," she says, then runs off to play.

Coolsville

Coltrane took a midnight train through bebop rains on his way to Coolsville.

Dylan was willin' to ride wild-word winds, singin' his way to Coolsville.

Audre Lorde never kneeled before any latchkey lackeys on her way to Coolsville.

Anna May Wong never gave her Hollywood star to anyone or anything but Coolsville.

While rioting his guitar, Hendrix ignited the smooth waters of Coolsville.

Rosa Parks never parked her courage anywhere but in the front seat of Coolsville.

If Books Powered Automobiles

I'd have a Bukowski wagon, a Didion pickup.

My vehicle would rant Corso and Wanda Coleman when speeding
down freeways. Meditate upon Rumi and Gwendolyn Brooks
when idling at red lights.

Kerouac and Carolyn Cassady for road trips. Joy Harjo combustion.

When stuck in L.A. traffic, my car could trade summer reading
lists with your car. Maybe I could add a few more memoirs to my
mileage, some Proust for a tune-up.

Machines running on James Joyce or David Foster Wallace would
get 100 mpg.

Banned books would fuel hot-rod rebel racers.

All vehicles, regardless of make or model, would be considered
smart cars.

Shakespeare's Scissors

I've got a dependable car but would rather travel at the speed of my dreams.

I have the apocalypse in my back pocket but want heaven on the telephone.

I've moshed to Gwar but prefer dancing in the park with my daughter.

I've got a candle in the wind but desire a burning ring of fire.

I have an excellent hairdresser but often wish for Shakespeare's scissors
to shear myself.

I've got GPS on my phone but fancy the internal compass of a blackbird.

I've got a dog in the race but sometimes long for a cat nap.

You

You're the gasoline fueling my heart machine.

You're the home sweet home giving voice to my battered microphone.

You're the sonata serenading my medulla oblongata.

You're the Xanadu paradising my don't-know-what-to-do.

You're the epiphany giving shine to my dim-bulb blues.

You're the pretty muse inspiring my sweet yoo-hoos.

Mona Lisa's Blue Eyes

admire Justin Timberlake's blue eyes.

Justin Timberlake's blue eyes croon to the spirit of Marvin Gaye.

The bullet in Marvin Gaye weeps heavy tears because it still doesn't understand why the father shot the son.

Sylvia Plath's depression runs its fingers through Walt Whitman's beard.

Wanda Coleman's rage dances on a dull day job's grave.

Langston Hughes' subtle stache drops acid with Dali's long lip hair.

Frida Kahlo's blue-green eyes start an art-rock band.

Her band goes on tour, thorns and hummingbirds the world, sings wings instead of worry, wings instead of stones, wings instead of weariness.

Frida Kahlo's eyes consider Mona Lisa's eyes.

This Is the Street

This is the street where I was born into a cradle of shadows
and thorns, where crowbars and crow bones were my teething toys.

This is the street where my tongue was turned to smoke,
where I spoke in the vocabulary of first-person perished.

This is the street where I'd pick through the rags and bones
of old alphabets, searching for words to call my own.

This is the street where the language of seekers, dreamers,
believers, and fire breathers came along one day.

They made me one of their own. Taught me how to finally clear
the tombstone outta my throat.

The Human Heart Is

Built from lion roar, broken crayons, raindrops, and amp feedback.

A denizen of ghost stories, all-night diners, and passing trains.

Rebellious, regal, filled with willows and wild-horse glory.

Beastmaster and dancemaker.

Creator of carnal conjurings, alchemist of strengths and sorrows from inexplicable sources.

Possessed of a voice born of big-bang karaoke. It growls, howls, and lullabies with lustral love light.

Given veins that pulse drumbeats and the sweet and sour of the midnight hour.

Assembled with sage, stardust, and spacejunk from all corners of the universe. It hangs like a lamp light within our chests and guides us forward.

Travels through the dark and light and back again.

Here, There, Everywhere

I asked far too many questions in Whynot, Mississippi.

Had loads of ambivalence in Uncertain, Texas.

First learned to kiss in Sweet Lips, Tennessee.

Felt like I never fit in there in Tightsqueeze, Virginia.

Sought transcendence in Sublimity, Oregon.

Escaped the rain in Waterproof, Louisiana.

Studied karma in Kismet, Kansas.

Watched the flowers propagate in Humptulips, Washington.

I was well fed in Bread Loaf, Vermont and Sandwich, New Hampshire.

Got way too hydrated in Chugwater, Wyoming, and way too caffeinated in Hot Coffee, Mississippi.

From Dull, Ohio, I roamed to Normal, Illinois, then landed in Mystic, Connecticut.

It was in Harmony, Minnesota I finally found my voice.

On Being a Father After 50

We compare ourselves
to George Clooney, James Earl Jones,
Elton John, and Mick Jagger.
Not because we're rock stars or movie stars
but because they, like us,
have entered fatherhood later in life.

When we were born into our new lives
as fathers after 50, our first words
out of the womb were:

I'm finally ready.

We've had years to unlearn
how our fathers taught us to bind our neckties
into chokeholds and how playdates
could include affairs
with the next-door neighbor.

We're calmer, wear our zen on our sleeves.
3:30 a.m. diaper disasters, no big deal.
We get to play peekaboo, tag,
and follow the leader.
We delight in snacks
like Goldfish crackers, juice boxes,
and apple slices.

We fathers after 50
get to teach language and learn it anew,
marvel at how letters like *d* and *a*
can build such a remarkable word as *dad*.

If we're older natural fathers,
we worry about our sperm count.
Chromosomal abnormalities. Autism. Schizophrenia.

If we're adoptive fathers,
we pass along the best of our DNA
through grace, empathy, and compassion.

If we're divorced fathers,
we only see our children on weekends,
hear them call someone else dad,
suffer the scraps of being a part-time parent
on a full-time love. Still, there's the equation
where two fathers equal double the love.
And if some pride must be swallowed
to impress that upon our children,
so be it.

We fathers after 50
wonder what our kids think about
having an older dad,
do they wonder how their fathers
may have missed out
on that Big Gulp at the fountain of youth.

We realize we are not Kevlar-coated.
It takes longer to heal from waterslides
and chasing our kids
who dart off on scooters and bikes.
We develop strategies
to gracefully rise from the floor
after playing with Legos.

At night, between diaper changes,
late-night feedings,
and the odd hours of sleep
with our significant other,
we sneak out to graveyards
and write on our future tombstones,

"Not ready to be here anytime soon."

Love Up

Our mothers
have gifted us with our first breath
and death will take our last.
Between those moments,
we're so many things—

cradle, cosmos, convicts in our skin.

We romp, we stomp, we bark and lark.
We slip, we slide, we kiss and cry,
sparkle and choir, shadow and fire
in all the ways love burns.

Rise and shine. Shine your rise. Up the love. Love up.

Love is feather-footed,
a rumble and tumble-jumble.
A radio oasis,
a dance floor float along.
Love is the starting whistle at the honey factory.
A groove, a mood, a bad tattoo removed,
an ocean of devotion with a watermark of wow.

Rise and shine. Shine your rise. Up the love. Love up.

Voice is love's voltage to energize and empower our lives.
With a well-honed noun or verb,
we can sweep someone off their feet.
But when adjectives turn tragic,
we're swept under the rug.

Sometimes we speak in hushed tones
when reciting poems, prayers, or lullabying a child.
I like it when we're loud,
when we sound like gasoline saints
in the combustible church of cool.

Rise and shine. Shine your rise. Up the love. Love up.

Bring back the troubled and addicted,
those who've fallen despair first
into the pill or whisky bottle.

Bring back the devasted and immolated,
those who've leapt from bridges and hotel balconies,
believing such a sudden exit from existence
was the only way to live.

Bring back the war-dead and disease-stricken.
The homeless and impoverished,
traumatized children and their broken mothers.
Anyone who has ever been shipwrecked by affection.

Rise and shine. Shine your rise. Up the love. Love up.

All you misfits and singers,
street sweepers and wisdom seekers.
The voiceless and choiceless,
truth deniers and doom defiers,
the opulent and oppressed.
Overworked nurses and armchair numismatists,
rock collectors and rock guitarists,
those whose inner child
has ever suffered from a bad hair day.

Shake off your chains, strip outta your doubts.
Open your doors, your hearts.

Come down off your mountains, emerge from the underground.
Fill your pockets with love's many syllables
so we may discover brighter,
more beautiful ways
to be.

Rise and shine. Shine your rise. Up the love. Love up.
Love shine. Shine your tune. Up rise. Heart bloom.
Peace up. Love the up. Love your voice. Love your shine.
Rise and shine. Shine your rise. Up the love. Love up.

She's Out There on the Highway

Somewhere between New York and North Carolina.

She's got her eyes on the road and her head in a radio melody.

The sun is high; her window's down. She feels the wind in her hair,
feels the freedom of roaming highways where no one knows
her name.

She's heard the blues bleed from a broken mirror. In her rearview,
a guitar tuned to the key of hurt is fading.

There's a lucky penny under her tongue; all her kisses taste of
wishing-water fountains.

Come evening, she'll pull off the road, maybe somewhere in
Virginia where love and death play double or nothing
with the moon's rent money.

The way the night's black dogs tell it, there's a little bit of wild
in everyone and everything.

Confetti Moon

Confetti moon
is pretty at a party,
twinkling lights falling all around.

She says you don't gotta
set yourself on fire
to experience illumination.
You don't have to
witness all the fresh scars
on the world's wrists
to know its sorrow.

Confetti moon don't mind
working the graveyard shift.
She don't mind
being the symphony conductor
of wolves and wild beasts.

She wears your nickname
on her tongue like a piercing.
Calls you sweetly
when you least expect it.
Confetti moon says
the hit parade don't have to hurt.

Ben Franklin's Kite

Deep within the dazzling storm behind your eyes,
I witness Ben Franklin's kite.

It loops, dips and rises, coaxes lightning from clouds.
My eyes mirror the flash of your eyes.

That's when you offer me
the electrically charged key to your heart.

Believe Me When I Say

If you ever felt locked into a timeshare along the River Styx.

Had your third eye stuck in the shop for repair.

Caught yourself in a mirror with a piece of grief stuck between your teeth.

Witnessed joy with rocks stuffed in its pockets, slouching towards the river.

If you ever had difficulty recognizing your genes from your jeans.

One too many high-fives from a sudden case of hives.

Had your imagination suddenly lose its penchant for tai chi and time travel.

Almost drowned while night swimming in a lake of good intentions.

Got stuck in a dive bar performing swan dives into a shot glass empty of salvation.

Believe me when I say joy has come to its senses. It's removed the rocks from its pockets, and it's heading straight toward you.

About the Author

L.A. poet/spoken-word performer Rich Ferguson has shared the stage with Patti Smith, Wanda Coleman, Moby, and other esteemed poets and musicians. He is a featured performer in the film, *What About Me?* featuring Michael Stipe, k.d. lang, and others. His poetry and award-winning spoken-word music videos have appeared in numerous anthologies and festivals. He is the author of the novel *New Jersey* Me (Rare Bird Books), and two poetry collections *8th & Agony* (Punk Hostage Press), and *Everything is Radiant Between the Hates* (Moon Tide Press). In 2022, he received an artist-in-residence grant from the Valparaiso Foundation in Spain. Most recently, Ferguson is the lead editor of an anthology of CA poets entitled *Beat Not Beat* (Moon Tide Press). He was selected by the National Beat Poetry Foundation, Inc. (NBPF), to serve as U.S. Beat Poet Laureate (Sept. 2023 to Sept. 2024).

Acknowledgements

These poems first appeared in the following publications:

A Picture Is Worth a Poet's Words: "Somewhere, a Playground"

The Sparring Artists/Sparring With Beatnik Ghosts #2: "3 AM Wafflehouse Waitresses"

Maintenant 19: "Dear America,"

Maintenant 18: "Open Letter to Human Existence"

Maintenant 17: "Once Again I Find Myself Wide Awake in This Bed"

Maintenant 16: "13 Ways of Looking at They"

Moon and Sun 13: "What I Confessed to Ophelia On Our First and Only Date"

From Venice to Venice: Poets of California and Italy / Da venice a venezia: Poeti e poete dalla california e italia: "What St. Christopher Told Me While Traveling Route 666", "What Good Conscience Says at the Dinner Table Between Mouthfuls of Light", "Ways to Write a Poem", "At 7th & Esperanza"

Look What I Did About Your Silence (an El Martillo Press Anthology): "The Superstitious Cemetery" and "The Feels"

Depose (an anthology of working class solidarity): "A Gene for Tears"

Huge and Heartfelt Thanks For Being You and Everything You Do:

To the Moon Tide Team: (Eric Morago, Michael Wada, Mackensi Green, Alyssa Murray, and Shelly Holder)

To My Brothers and Sisters in Poetic and Artful Arms (in no particular order): Bob Holman; Peter Carlaftes & Kat Georges at Three Rooms Press; Matt Sedillo & David A. Romero at El Martillo Press; Amy Gerstler, Derrick Brown, Bill Mohr & Luivette Resto (bless you beautiful blurbsters); S.A. Griffin (let's be sure to go down with the band on the U.S.S. Apocalypse), Michael C. Ford, Iris Berry, Mike M. Mollett, Richard Modiano & Daniel Yaryan; Quentin Ring, Jimmy Vega, Iván Salinas, Eric Ahlberg, Genesis Perez & the living spirit of Wanda Coleman at Beyond Baroque; Shirl Perl & Billy at Wacko; Mark Wilkinson (for cinematically supporting my work), the International Video Poetry Festival, Weimar Poetry Film Festival, REELpoetry/Houston, Lynn Moss Holley & the International Poetry Film Festival L.A., Monica Valdés, Cat Gwynn, Sarah Tremlett & Marc Zegans; Mark Lipman (kudos for sending poetry to the moon!), Jane Ormerod, Peter Darrell, David Lawton & George Wallace (gwfm will forever be in my heart), Deborah Tosun Kilday & Paul Richmond at the National Beat Poetry Foundation; Brett Hall Jones, Janet Fitch, Andrew Tonkovich, Lisa Alvarez & the Community of Writers; Alexis Rhone Fancher, Susan Hayden, Michelle Bitting, Phil Abrams, Lynne Thompson, Brendan Constantine, Harry E. Northup, Amy Raasch, Ron Koertge, Sharp-Eyed Amélie Frank, Patrick O'Neil, Syd Straw, Liz Foster, Celia Chavez & Simon Petty, Bernie Larsen & the Ojai Underground, Diana Faust, Christian Georgescu, Katherine Williams, Chloe Forkerway at Buxton Books, Elena Karina Byrne, Kim Shuck, Tongo Eisen-Martin, Alexandra Kostoulas & the SF Creative Writing Institute, Stephanie Barbé Hammer, Hilda Weiss & Wayne Lindberg, Valaparaiso Foundation in Spain for my residency, Ellyn Maybe, Elena Secota, Kim Ohanneson, Linda Kunik, Kelly Gray, Kathryn DeLancellotti, K.R. Morrison, Milo Martin & Keith Martin, Suzanne Thompson, Jerry the Priest, Jennifer Jesse Smith, Kennon B. Raines, Shana Nys Dambrot, Kathi Flood, the Sunday poetry workshop crew (Nicelle Davis, Aruni Wijesinghe, Alexandra Umlas, Jeremy Ra, Nancy Beagle, Terri Niccum, Elaine Mintzer, Julissa Cardenas, Patti Scruggs, P.K., Jesse James & Mackensi Green), Finn Taylor, Jeremy Toback, Butch Norton, Andrew Bush, David Sutton, Joe Kara, James Morrison, Alex Frankel, Don Kingfisher Campbell, Gary Justice, Suzy Williams, Bill Burnett, Gerry Fialka, Annie Wood, Eric Vollmer, Veronica Jauregui, Alan Rifkin, Jeff Rogers, Frédéric Iriarte,

Dave Essinger, Dorothy Orant Morrison, Michele Joseph, Merle Brezianu, Chris Ellis, John Moody, The Pondwater Family (RIP King Daddy), Mauro Monteiro (RIP).

To My Father and Brother: Thank you for your continued love and support, even when I was a complete screwup.

To My Three Outside Hearts: my wife Kathleen Florence, my daughter Evelyn Everything, and Mother Mary. Thank you for your continued love, support, inspiration, and for helping birth and rebirth my creative imagination.

Also Available from Moon Tide Press

*Sh!t Men Say to Me: A Poetry Anthology in Response
to Toxic Masculinity* (2021)
Flower Grand First, Gustavo Hernandez (2021)
Everything is Radiant Between the Hates, Rich Ferguson (2020)
When the Pain Starts: Poetry as Sequential Art, Alan Passman (2020)
This Place Could Be Haunted If I Didn't Believe in Love,
Lincoln McElwee (2020)
Impossible Thirst, Kathryn de Lancellotti (2020)
Lullabies for End Times, Jennifer Bradpiece (2020)
Crabgrass World, Robin Axworthy (2020)
Contortionist Tongue, Dania Ayah Alkhouli (2020)
The only thing that makes sense is to grow, Scott Ferry (2020)
Dead Letter Box, Terri Niccum (2019)
Tea and Subtitles: Selected Poems 1999-2019, Michael Miller (2019)
At the Table of the Unknown, Alexandra Umlas (2019)
The Book of Rabbits, Vince Trimboli (2019)
Everything I Write Is a Love Song to the World, David McIntire (2019)
Letters to the Leader, HanaLena Fennel (2019)
Darwin's Garden, Lee Rossi (2019)
Dark Ink: A Poetry Anthology Inspired by Horror (2018)
Drop and Dazzle, Peggy Dobreer (2018)
Junkie Wife, Alexis Rhone Fancher (2018)
The Moon, My Lover, My Mother, & the Dog, Daniel McGinn (2018)
Lullaby of Teeth: An Anthology of Southern California Poetry (2017)
Angels in Seven, Michael Miller (2016)
A Likely Story, Robbi Nester (2014)
Embers on the Stairs, Ruth Bavetta (2014)
The Green of Sunset, John Brantingham (2013)
The Savagery of Bone, Timothy Matthew Perez (2013)
The Silence of Doorways, Sharon Venezio (2013)
Cosmos: An Anthology of Southern California Poetry (2012)
Straws and Shadows, Irena Praitis (2012)
In the Lake of Your Bones, Peggy Dobreer (2012)
I Was Building Up to Something, Susan Davis (2011)
Hopeless Cases, Michael Kramer (2011)
One World, Gail Newman (2011)
What We Ache For, Eric Morago (2010)

Now and Then, Lee Mallory (2009)
Pop Art: An Anthology of Southern California Poetry (2009)
In the Heaven of Never Before, Carine Topal (2008)
A Wild Region, Kate Buckley (2008)
Carving in Bone: An Anthology of Orange County Poetry (2007)
Kindness from a Dark God, Ben Trigg (2007)
A Thin Strand of Lights, Ricki Mandeville (2006)
Sleepyhead Assassins, Mindy Nettifee (2006)
Tide Pools: An Anthology of Orange County Poetry (2006)
Lost American Nights: Lyrics & Poems, Michael Ubaldini (2006)

Patrons

Moon Tide Press would like to thank the following people for their support in helping publish the finest poetry from the Southern California region. To sign up as a patron, visit www.moontidepress.com or send an email to publisher@moontidepress.com.

Anonymous
Robin Axworthy
Conner Brenner
Nicole Connolly
Bill Cushing
Susan Davis
Kristen Baum DeBeasi
Peggy Dobreer
Kate Gale
Dennis Gowans
Alexis Rhone Fancher
HanaLena Fennel
Half Off Books & Brad T. Cox
Donna Hilbert
Jim & Vicky Hoggatt
Michael Kramer
Ron Koertge & Bianca Richards
Gary Jacobelly
Ray & Christi Lacoste

Jeffery Lewis
Zachary & Tammy Locklin
Lincoln McElwee
David McIntire
José Enrique Medina
Michael Miller & Rachanee Srisavasdi
Michelle & Robert Miller
Ronny & Richard Morago
Terri Niccum
Andrew November
Jeremy Ra
Luke & Mia Salazar
Jennifer Smith
Roger Sponder
Andrew Turner
Rex Wilder
Mariano Zaro
Wes Bryan Zwick

www.ingramcontent.com/pod-product-compliance
Lightning Source LLC
Chambersburg PA
CBHW031142090426
42738CB00008B/1186